BREATHE INTO THE BONES

Saffron Coomber

Presentation by BookLeaf Publishing

Web: www.bookleafpub.com

E-mail: info@bookleafpub.com

ISBN: 9789358360905

First edition 2021

For all those who have felt powerless

For all those who have been silenced

For all those who burn with rage

For all those who drown in grief

For all those who feel alone

For all those who feel everything

And for my mother, Patricia Maureen Coomber, who loved with ferocity.

ACKNOWLEDGEMENTS

My purest gratitude goes to my friends and family who have inspired every stage of transformation.

Dad, Saskia, Ethan, and Leigh- you saved me when our world ended. I love you.

Thank you to my angels on earth who have borne witness whilst I've laughed, cried, and fell apart. I wouldn't have the words today without you in my life. Thank you for listening to me. Thank you for leading me. Thank you for helping me find my voice. You know who you are. I love you.

Thank you to the ancestors, for my life. Thank you that I still hear the call of the Wild. Thank you to every moment of being alive. Both pain and pleasure have birthed this book. I love you.

And thank you to whomever takes the time to read these words. I hope they offer you something. I love you.

PREFACE

Little One

Just write it down

Take all you have

Pour it onto the page

And let your soul speak.

Come to the feast

All may enter here

Take a bite out of

Bursting thighs

Sink teeth into

Willing flesh

Ignore the shriek

Escaping the gorged

Mouth

Crack open the ribs

Drink the spine

Pierce bruised skin

And

Rip

Me

To

Shreds.

Then

When all's done

With last night's sacrament still dripping from your

chin There is nothing left

But to heave my steaming carcass

And throw me to the dogs.

2

I peer over the precipice of my heart

And Truth glares back.

I can see resentment in the hollows of her

cheeks She knows what's coming.

Eyes wide, she stares.

Accusing.

So weak from neglect

Emaciated through disrespect,

'Feed me,' she mouths.

A challenge.

But once again

My back has already turned

Lids firmly shut

I trip blindly away

Leaving nothing but lies in my wake.

I am stood

Shivering at the banks of Life

Elbows grasped, knees

knocking Held

So

Tight.

'Give it to the Water,'

The Ancestors whisper.

I gaze defiantly at Her

Chin up, jaw clenched

Held

So

Tight.

'Give it to the Water.'

I see my reflection in Her face

Recognition shimmers across Her

eyes Gently,

She waves.

'Come, my child

Lay your head at my breast

And take a drink.'

Cautiously I step

One toe following another

Into Her depths

Warm

Inviting

Still.

'Give it to the Water.'

I'm up to my neck and I can't

stand Arms flail, legs kick

There is nothing holding me

now She fills my lungs

And

I

Sink.

So full of Water am I

I do not know where She ends and I

begin Her tears mingle with mine

As I choke up Shame

I am engulfed

In Rage

I sear

With Pain

As storms surge in my veins

Her blood boils

And I

Am

Spent.

8

Soon,

There is calm.

She wrings the salt from my

hair Lapping kisses lick my

face Her arms surround me

and I am held

So tight.

It's the small things

That make Life

Mighty

Precious moments

So minute

They fit in the wink of an eye

An intake of Breath

Every time your heart

Beats.

So much Life

And yet so small

Maybe I don't need to be so big after all.

What is it about me,

Standing no higher than five feet,

That makes them so weak?

I am not talking about knees

Buckling willingly to fall prostrate with

ease But rather

Running

And hiding

Blinding their eyes

To their imminent demise.

You forget

I can smell the terror in your blood

I can taste the cold sweat trickling down your

neck I can follow you into the fire and pass

unscathed Whilst your courage turns to dust.

I wonder

If under

All that man

All *this* woman

Reveals the boy you really are?

Sometimes

All it takes

Is a little tenderness

A little gentleness

The greatest intimacy

Lies in the eyes

Meeting soul to soul

To be soft takes great

strength You should try it

sometime Like Otis says

A little tenderness.

Something beautiful happened today

And my Mother celebrates.

The trees whisper their excitement

The tulips open their mouths in delight

Giggling out their heady scent

The Wind teases my hair

Coyly wrapping each curl around Her fingers

Whilst the Sun turns Her beaming face to me

Winking conspiratorially with each languorous

cloud Something beautiful happened today

And my Mother celebrates.

I pick up my crown

Adorn my brow

And allow myself

To feel proud.

I give away

So much of myself

It's a wonder

I see anything at all

When I look in the mirror.

It is enough

To simply

Eat

When you are hungry

Sleep

When you are tired

Cry

When you are sad.

Do not let the idea of how you should do these

things Stop you

From simply being

Enough.

No man's arms

Have ever matched

The strength of my

mother's. She who held me

Even before birth

Scooping me up after

every Fall

Disgrace

Heartbreak.

She who cleared my

face of Food

Tears

Fear.

She whose fingers found my hair

And soothed my troubled locks

Into flowing tributaries.

My mother's love was

A chrysalis

A talisman

Protection I wore daily without even knowing it.

But now

With the hag's stone cracked

And the still-wet wings plucked

I am laid bare

At the mercy of ghouls

And their grinning grasp.

Romanticize yourself

Comb your hair with the patience of a

Siren Perched atop her rock

Drinking in her reflection in the depths below.

Anoint yourself

With the devotion of a Priestess

Let holy oils cascade down

The undulations of your Temple.

Caress yourself

With the hands of Aphrodite

Discover deliciousness in all the

places You wish they'd dare touch.

Bathe yourself

In the sound of your own Pleasure

Do not wait for Life to offer its

hand Understand that power

Preys between your palms.

Sometimes

When we are gripping so

hard Onto what was

It comes as a surprise

Once we unfurl our unwilling

fist That there was nothing

there To begin with.

Sadness

Pinches my heart to see if I'm

awake As she clambers behind

my eyes

Suffocating them

With overbearing enthusiasm

We watch

Streams wind their way down my

face Marvelling at the salt crystals

Clutching my lashes

She visits me often

Yet turns up unannounced

On her arrival I am waiting for her

departure Unwelcome and welcome both

For

She is the one who sits with me in grief

She tends to the ravaged ruins of my

heart She forces no words when I wish

to be silent

But when I wish to howl

She is right there with me

Cracking her own voice

In solidarity.

If they tell you

That you are

'Too much'

They have merely caught their

reflection In the Truth of your Eye

And resent to find

That in fact

It is them

Who is not enough.

Imma go off for a minute

Y'all hate on hairless cats

Until it comes to pussy

I know we are animals

But we skin those we want to eat

And need I remind you

I AM NOT A PIECE OF MEAT

You want me to strip the womanhood from my

body To reflect the girl I was

Inspect that:

If you prefer the look of a *child*

Then move along, sir,

You are too young to ride.

My friend once told me

In my past life I was burnt at the

stake For all the fire I carry with me

now.

Perhaps that is why when I try

To speak

Ancient smoke scorches my throat

Bitter ash falls familiar on my tongue

And forgotten flames still writhe beneath my feet.

Many look at tears

With the mocking disdain

Of weakness

Softness

Hysteria.

Yet see how you laugh

When the Sky opens her Gates of Grief

Soaking you in Her suffering

When the Sea

Seeing red

Seethes in tsunamis

When the River

Releases her Wrath on those who would

contain Her Water is at once

Life-giver and Life-taker

Be warned

When you see my tears

fall They are merely

leaks

Of the teeming tempests

below Dangerous enough

To drown us both.

I saw you in the sky today

Your double rainbow grin

Stopping me in my tracks

Calling my own smile to greet

yours. I know you were happy to

see me For your droplets of

gratitude Mingled with mine

And went

Hand in hand

Caressing the curve of my cheeks.

So many women live in me

Entities untold but those who visit

most Are the ghost of my mother

The one who brings the

Wilderness The watchful Eye of

the Angel And most recently

My little girl

Kept hidden in the dark

So cold she is

Would these women work

together To draw her out

Warm the numb limbs

Kiss the frozen mouth

Breathe into the bones

And guide her into the light.

If you find

You're knelt

At another's table

Having not even been offered a seat

And are gladly accepting

The scraps they drop

From their overflowing plate

You pick yourself up from under their

opinion Dust the unworthiness from your

knees

Collect the cracks of your dignity

Enter your own kitchen

And eat.

- Do not let anyone dictate whether you are satisfied or starving

Call me a trapeze artist

The way I pendulum swing

between Self-loathing and love.

Watch me cut arcs of indecision in the

air Freewheeling through hoops of

truth And webs of lies

I teeter on the tight rope of

growth Hold your breath

One wrong move and I will surely fall

Or perhaps

There is a chance

That I may soar.

It stings to know

After all the times of

choosing Them

It has never been

Me

Though it shouldn't be a

surprise Even with myself

I am always picked last.

When I look at my hands

And my nails are long

I see they belong to my mother

Other times

I follow the heartlines to my

grandmother It is a small comfort

To know when I feel

Alone

Those I carry with me

Are as far as my fingertips.

Befriend your Rage

She is your messenger against

mistreatment Heed them no more

When they say

Too much of Her

Results in

Too much of You

You know She's coming

When She simmers at the base of your

spine You feel the hot flush

As she rakes her claws against your flesh in

blush Let your nostrils flare with hers

And release your dragon's breath

Show your TEETH

Let your fangs DRIP

With venomous justice

It is understood

That even Hell cannot match

When Fury partners us in

Scorn Therefore

She is your greatest ally

Your sister in arms

Follow Her

Roaring into bloody battle

Raise your torch to the ancestral

fires And set the world ablaze.

At 3:30

In the dark of the hour

Loneliness slips through my

window Slides in beside me

And wakes me up.

She presses her toes against my

calves Stealing my breath with her

chill She chuckles as she frosts

my neck Freezing me in place

As she warms her palms

Against my heart

I can only observe.

We lay for so long in this

way Sometimes I am

surprised

My pulse is still present

Sometimes

It hammers against its cage

Attempting to escape this finger

trap Demanding to take futile

flight.

There is felicity in this fight

For when she is done

And the Sun finally comes to my

defence She deserts me

Victorious

Draped with stolen strength

Whilst I

Wrung dry

Am a crumpled mass

In soaking sheets.

The words aren't coming

today My stomach hurts

And my heart is a box

I follow thoughts

Racing through warrens

Delving into dens

But in the end

The sentence

Slips through the net

And I am left

Desperate for sense.

It's overcrowded inside my body

So many voices I can barely discern my

own Conversations replayed

Analysed

And ultimately despised

Relentless resurrections of

Should haves

Would haves

Could haves

Memories of monsters

Haunt Halls of Regret

There is not a lot of space here these

days Not even for me.

What a privilege it is

To hold Love in my arms

To feel its weight

His head rested on my

shoulder So safe with me

That sleep nestles in his

breath Gently in and out

As our heartbeats sway in

sync Our first meeting

And here we are holding each

other We both offer gifts

Mine of protection

And his

This tiny body

Grounds me.

My heart is a battering ram

Against the dam of self-control

I am on

EDGE

My feet stand splayed

Stock still

I can feel the fissures start to groan As

pressure swells below the surface

Glacial tears travelling the ends of my

wits Something is coming

And coming soon

I will burst

Head second, heart first.

My heart is my most used muscle

I've thrown it into the ring so many

times And so many times it returns

A battered, bleeding pulp

I trace its outlines

The scars, the welts, the wounds

Torn apart and patched together so

often It is almost unrecognizable

It is no new and shiny thing

It has seen war

Stood in naked offering

Maimed before my eyes with weaponous

words And decimated

At the decease

Of my mother.

This heart of mine is old

Weather-worn

A beast of burden

And yet

To me

She beats with dignity

Honouring those who gave her a

chance To feel.

There are so many things I wish I could tell you.

Small things, like:

I got my vaccination today and I didn't cry when the needle
went in

I am growing up

I know you'd be proud because I am proud of myself. My

orchid has a fresh bloom with other buds waiting their

turn.

Big things, like:

The work I've got coming up

Just to see the light in your eyes

And your smile spreading like the sunbeam you

are To see me do well.

How much I miss you on days like this

In such familiar places

The sun is shining

Everything is bright

People laugh as their lives go on

On days like this

Without you

I don't feel the heat like I used to

Smells of summer seem more bitter

than sweet

And my laugh?

Cavernous

Echoing against the emptiness

Where you should be.

32

I saw myself in a dream once

Standing before my person

Royal in a purple dress

Hair a halo

With silver slivers of the moon

Luminous in my eyes.

I wore a smile I had not seen in my waking

life I held myself with all the acceptance of

What was

What is

And what will be.

I took up space

Knowing my place in the

universe Was non-negotiable.

An understanding so

clear I could only see

With both eyes wide shut.

33

I am of the Old Ways

Give me fire, woodsmoke, heat

Let the rain saturate my every pore

And clothe me in a way that cloth cannot

Let me taste the salt on my tongue

As I delve into the depths of our Blue

Mother And have the wisdom to listen

When She tells me to leave

Before Her love engulfs me

May the wind tangle my hair with ancient hands

May I tread lightly where the sweet earth kisses my

feet I carry the cosmos in me

There are nebulas in my eyes

Galaxies between my thighs

And when I move this body to frenzy

You better believe

That every watching star in

heaven Is finally set free.

34

I drag the past behind me as if my life depended

on it A torturous tether to cautionary tales of

Being I was lost in the woods

Facing my own wolves

And perishing in the act.

Along the way

I convinced myself that these spectres of experience
keep me connected

To who I could be

But rather they keep me closed to

Who I am.

To every person

Still in the forest

Grappling with demons unspeakable

Know the fight is already won:

Lay down your armour

Shed the skins you cloak your Self in

Remember the breadcrumbs you placed along

the way And follow your path

Home.

I hope you can thank

yourself For every version

of you

I am learning how

To recall past selves with

welcome Rather than rebuke.

Now

I am willing to listen

Find compassion

And embrace

Where before I would

Deface.

These little lives

Have led me to where I am

today So many brave girls

Come and gone

I hope if I get to be old

I will hold this present incarnation

fondly Smooth my furrowed brow

Offer laughing libations

Lift my trembling chin

Assuring,

'Your only task was to live

It is not a sin.'

36

54

There is no fear of the dark when you are the light.

www.ingramcontent.com/pod-product-compliance
Lightning Source LLC
LaVergne TN
LVHW021238200726

843509LV00012B/1517